The Apple Tree Theory
The Entrepreneur's Guide to Success

by
Niklas Alm

The Apple Tree Theory

Copyright © 2021 by Niklas Alm

All Rights Reserved. No part of this book may be reproduced or transmitted in any form or by any means, graphic, electronic, or mechanical, including photocopying, recording, taping, or by any information storage retrieval system, without the written permission of the author.

Third Edition published April 2021

Cover design by Cindy Anderson

Why did I write this book?

Simply put, because I think I have found a recipe, a cure or a plan if you will. Which actually works. For some reason, I want to get this out of me. Sometimes I think it's to explain to my daughter how I work and have worked and sometimes I think it's to help others I write. But honestly, I'm not really sure, which also feels perfectly ok. I just know I have to publish this book.

To my daughter

I am immensely grateful that you are in my life, Linn.
You are my purpose, my meaning, and my absolute everything.
There is nothing that competes with you.
No galaxies, gods, or other desires.
You are everything to me and I love you unconditionally.
I do not believe in a god in a specific form, name, or icon, but I do not make less of the power that many believe in; that force which transcends everything and that creates everything. The true divine power, and the one that brought you into my life.
When we die, I hope we will meet again in Nangijala and that we will live there for an eternity with all our friends.

Nightie-nightie, sweet dreams.
Daddy loves you most in the whole world.
You are my best friend.
I am proud of you.
I will see you tomorrow.

Definition of entrepreneur
: one who organizes, manages, and assumes the risks of a business or enterprise
(Merriam Webster Dictionary)

The word *entrepreneur* comes from *enterprise*, which is commonly defined as ***an undertaking, something attempted***; but what is interesting is the ultimate root of the word, which is from French, ***entre*** (in or between) and ***prendre*** (to take).
So, by its very nature as a word, it clearly suggests that ***entrepreneurs take challenges***

Picture this…

An apple tree, where every apple you pluck and bite into, endows you with more knowledge about life, some principle or law that can be applied to achieve greater success and happiness.

How many apples would you pick and eat from that tree?

Most of us are looking for those apples, the answers that will give us the means of achieving success, happiness, and security in our lives, and that is exactly what this book is all about.

This book is a compilation of what you might find if you ate from that tree; a collection of theories, laws, and principles, some of them based on my own experience and observations as an entrepreneur, and many of them borrowed from others. Like the apples on this tree of knowledge, each section I present to you will give you some sense of how to become more successful in life – which can be measured by your happiness and of course, your financial status.

I spent many years studying the area of entrepreneurship and how to achieve success, and having had my own success as an entrepreneur, I have had some insights about what I think is important and what I can offer to others.

This is not a religious text. I do not espouse any God or belief system. What I present here is observable and requires your observation, not your unquestioning belief.

The book is presented in short and easily assimilated passages, each one detailing a certain theory, law, or principle of life. There is no attempt to show how they work, or how you should go about applying them in your life – that is a matter of personal application and observation. You will learn what works for you by using it and seeing the results.

Some of the material I present is certainly open for discussion, and some are so obvious that they cannot be challenged, like gravity, but all of them are based on perceptible fundamentals or truths.

Try reading at least one or two of the short chapters each night before going to sleep. Let it soak into your consciousness, maybe even dream about it, and then wake up with a different perspective, an expanded one, where you start to see fantastic new possibilities and potential in the world.

But make no mistake about it, just reading this book will not be enough – you will need to put the material to practice. Any successful entrepreneur will tell you that it takes a lot more than wishful thinking to reach the mountain top. It takes discipline, daily application, and not luck or hopeful wishes. The Universe does not just hand it all to you – you need to make the Universe play ball with you.

Enjoy the read and good luck to you.

Niklas Alm

The Apple Tree Theory

Let us take a scenario to illustrate the fundamentals of the Apple Tree Theory in application, on a purely pragmatic level.

You own a house and property with a well-manicured lawn that the boy next door mows for you once a week at a rate of $10 per hour, twenty times a year. Assuming it takes him an hour each time, the annual cost of doing so = $200.

At some point you decide to purchase some apple trees and shrubs to make your property look more attractive. You plant them around the perimeter of the lawn. The cost of purchasing them = $150.

Now that you've planted trees and shrubs, the time required to mow the lawn increases by an extra thirty minutes, due to the fact that it takes longer to navigate around trees and shrubs and requires that the boy go back with trimmers afterwards to get to the areas he couldn't reach with the mower. Add to this expense, increased costs in gasoline, clippers, parts, repairs, etc. and you have added a minimum of $150 to the annual cost of upkeeping the lawn.

One day, the boy's father decides that he no longer wants to lend out his personal lawn mower because it is causing wear and tear to his machine. You are forced to purchase a lawn mower at a cost of $500. This becomes a recurring cost every seven years or so.

Other hidden costs include purchasing shears, rakes, trimmers for the shrubs, fertilizer and seeding for the grass, and the costs continue to go up.

Extrapolate this scenario, assuming you remain in the same house for at least forty years, and we see that the simple act of planting those trees and shrubs will have cost you around $6000 in materials and an estimated 1900+ hours of work to maintain. 1900 hours is more than most people have in working hours for a whole year, including working holidays. If you hired someone to do this work, you would have paid out $8500 (based on current monetary values) in maintenance.

On the other hand, instead of spending that extra money on the lawn what if had you invested it more smartly? You would have seen considerably more returns by the end of that forty-year period – that is clear.

Of course, if gardening is high on your life's priority list, then the costs are an acceptable value. If gardening is not on your priority list of fun things to do, and you simply want to keep your property well-maintained, then you lost an enormous amount of time and money by adding those trees and shrubs; and that is time and money that will be deducted from the things you really wanted to do and accomplish in your life.

With this scenario in mind, let us look at another approach, one which, in the long-run, would achieve a similar result – a manicured lawn that is also aesthetic, but which does not detract from achieving your dreams.

With this perspective in mind, you take another road, you do some research, and you find some plants which require zero maintenance, and you also find out that you can place stone sculptures and other aesthetic pieces around the property which make it attractive to the eye and are virtually maintenance free – and to that end, nearly cost-free for years to come. The money and time you saved go towards your more priority goals.

If you view your life in this way, if you prioritize your expenses and budget, you can still get the pleasure and joy and aesthetics you want, but without undue burden, and more importantly, without derailing what is most important to you.

Advice:
Think carefully about things which incur long-term running costs. Will they empower your goals or detract from them?

Eye-opener:
You can either spend your money on the garden or invest it smartly and end up with more money in the end.

When a little becomes GREAT

There is a saying, *"If it isn't broke, don't fix it"*.

This can be applied to anything in life which is working reasonably well; why bother changing it? The logic is simple; if there are better results to be seen by changing it, the profit would still be quite modest as it was already working well enough.

The opposite side of the coin is the theory of *the broken window*; one that is widely accepted and used in behavioral research. Here is an actual example of this theory in application.

A nice residential area becomes the target of random graffiti. If this is not addressed immediately, it will degrade the value of the entire residential zone, attracting negative energy in the form of more graffiti, and certainly crime. The whole area is at risk of declining.

The *"broken window theory"* has its roots in New York City, when, some years back, the city was experiencing a wave of rising crime. As part of its battle against crime, the city administration adopted a simple approach: every time graffiti appeared, they promptly cleaned it up. That, along with other measures, reduced crime by half over a period of several years.

What is implied by the "*broken window theory*" is that even the smallest details can have great impact and long-term consequences.

To appreciate the power of this theory, one must take the longer view, not the short one. Focusing on such small details can seem pointless in the face of larger issues, missing the fact that a small ripple can become a large wave with far-reaching effects. This theory is somewhat parallel to the "*the butterfly effect*" – which will be discussed later in this book.

Advise:

Be very vigilant about even the smallest details concerning your life. Small changes can have huge effects.

Eye-opener:

If the crime rate of an entire city can be drastically reduced by addressing graffiti, what is required to start changing your life?

Freedom

How does freedom relate to success?

We all want it – but how exactly does freedom factor in to achieving success in life?

Here is how I see it, if you are not free enough to see outside the box of your current life, you will not be receptive to the opportunities which are there.

The question is, do you feel free in your life?

To that question, most people will answer – *yes*.

However, pause a little and think about it; is that an honest answer for you?

Are you free to do whatever you want and when you want?

Are you truly open to all possibilities?

Are you free when someone dictates how much you make in salary and when you get your vacation?

Are you free when you rely on other people to pay your pension?

These may seem like redundant points, but are they?

What does freedom really mean?

As a successful entrepreneur, I define freedom as – ***being able to do what you want when you want to.***

We start out free in life, with so much power of choice ahead of us. As children, growing up into youth and then young adults, we see opportunity all around us; we have not stepped into the box and closed the lids on ourselves. Eventually, however, as we lock ourselves into a career, with credit card debts, mortgages, familial responsibilities, our personal freedom seems to transform into a kind of collective bondage. It is not easy to go in the opposite direction of that collective mindset and one feels compelled to play the game before us.

To achieve the freedom I define above, you must be incredibly focused on everything that goes on in your life. It is vital that the people you surround yourself with (especially the partner you live with) do not burden you, but instead, lift you up. Real freedom, by definition, mandates that your life should not be dictated or shackled by others. Freedom is based on mutual love and agreement – not slavish conditions.

Why is freedom so difficult to comprehend?

"Things were easier in the past," a common utterance you hear from people – as if their lives were easier when they were younger. Was it really?

In the past, the great challenge to the culture was having enough food to survive. Living and life was largely centered around farming, food production and distribution. In our modern culture, this has all changed, because food distribution and availability has changed the terms of the game. Based on this alone, one could conclude that life is far easier today, and without the burden of having to grow and store our own food stocks, we are free to do the things we really want to. The question remains, what does one DO with that potential freedom?

I pose some simple questions to illustrate the point of freedom of choice.

Question: Can you go off tomorrow and do whatever you want?
Answer: No, I must work.
Question: Can you see yourself living your dream?
Answer: No, I must keep working to pay our mortgage and bills until the day I retire.

I could pose dozens of different scenarios, all of which would illustrate the fundamental problem; so long as you do not *feel* that YOU have the power of choice over your life, you will never take the leap to achieve those golden opportunities just waiting for you.

If you are so busy that you decline offers when friends or associates call on you, they will eventually stop calling.

If every opportunity that comes your way is simply shut down before it has a chance to develop into something, then eventually, you stop looking altogether.

The difference between those who succeed, and those who reach their financial dreams, is that they are receptive to new opportunities, and they jump at *"the chance of a lifetime"*. They are not afraid to take the leap of faith – and that is exercising their power of choice. If you are afraid to take chances, to walk down new roads of opportunity, if you do not have enough confidence or trust in your ability to do so, you are, to that degree, a prisoner of your own limitations – you are not free to make new choices in *your* life.

Advice:

Review your life and remove those things which are not high priority in terms of achieving your goals. This sounds easy, but it is more difficult than you can imagine. With determination and discipline, sometimes to the point of what others may see as absurd or even reckless, you will have made a big step toward becoming a happier and more successful individual.

Eye-opener:

If an acquaintance or friend offers you the opportunity to check out their investment model, should you, or should you not check it out?

What do you gain by doing so? What do you lose? Maybe there is an opportunity of a lifetime just waiting for you.

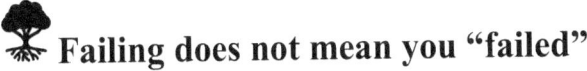 **Failing does not mean you "failed"**

The word "fail" comes from Latin, *fallere, to disappoint, deceive.*

The connotation of the word *failure* does not imply giving up, hopelessness, uselessness, unsuccessful or any other of a dozen modifiers. It just means, in essence, ***to disappoint***, and disappointment can disappear, like dust in the wind, in just seconds. It is impermanent.

There is a universal law to the effect that, *the more you try at something, the more likely you are to succeed*. This, like many other laws, is based on pure probability theory; like rolling the dice, the more times you turn the dice, the greater your chances are that the winning combination will eventually come up.

One can rewrite that law to the effect that, if one accumlates many failures, eventually, the learning curve will lead one to success. It suggests that failure is not an absolute, but rather, a road to eventual success. This may sound strange, but it is not.

Example:

You decide you are going to learn how to water ski. Statistically, a novice needs upwards of thirty-five attempts before they successfully negotiate the process. If you are not aware of this, you might decide, after just a few failed attempts, feeling embarrassed. Maybe even humiliated after landing on your face more times than you would care to, that water skiing is not for you. In fact, after roughly twenty attempts, most people give up, thinking, *I am too heavy, I have bad balance, etc.* They are simply trying to find a reason to justify the failure, when in fact, the only factual reason is that they failed to stick with it long enough to jump the learning-curve and succeed. Coming up with excuses for failure, not only puts up a roadblock to one's success, but it also lowers one's self-esteem, making future endeavors more difficult.

If you are aware of how "failure" factors in with success, you will not be so inclined to give up early in the process. With that perspective, performance anxiety is blown away and you can focus entirely on the task of getting up on those skis. I would venture to say that those who see "failure" as a learning curve to success, will probably get up on the skis before their 20th try.

Example:

When it comes to new start-ups, in whatever field, statistically, 1 in 10 will be successful.

This means that if you want to run your own business, you must be prepared to start about ten times before you succeed.

This might look like a hell of a mountain to climb, but it is, in fact, positive news! Instead of going around after the first failure and thinking that you are not competent or any such self-placating excuses, you have a platform, a law that permits you to mentally cope with it. If you failed the first time, you know that somewhere ahead lies success – just keep trying. Success favors those who do not quit.

Most athletes use this factor as a form of self-visualization to achieve great results. They see in their inner mind the perfect performance and they remind themselves that it is only a matter of time before they will achieve the results they are striving for. This is called self-affirmation – you are envisioning success, so eventually, the Universe will conform to your wishes.

Failure is not negative, it is positive. It is safe to try, and even in the face of failure, to keep going – because success is waiting for you somewhere up that road.

Advice:
Try new things, think of new ways to reach your goals, and put them to practice. Try, try, and try again. If you assume this mindset, I guarantee that you will achieve success in life. It is never fun to fail, but if you look at it as a bump in the road to your eventual success, then all that matters is that you keep going forward and keep your eye on the mountain top.

Eye-opener:
Did you learn to ride a bike on the first try?
How many times did you fall before you finally got it?

Cause and Effect

To achieve happiness and success it is important to understand that everything happens for a reason, and that luck, in the true meaning of the word, plays no factor in the plan you need to achieve your goals. Being "lucky", is more about having a well-developed attention to detail, and nothing to do with the winds of fate.

The universe is, as you know, made up of energies, energies which are indestructible, and yet controllable, and which can be converted into other energies. What is often overlooked when trying to achieve results, is the fact that the expenditure of small amounts of energy can play an incredibly large role in achieving BIG results. This is sometimes referred to as the *butterfly effect* or the *ripple effect*, where a small causation, like a stone dropped in a pond, ripples out and becomes a wave for change elsewhere.

Example:
IKEA did not become the world's largest furniture giant by chance. Ingvar Kamprad,

the founder, was looking for a niche where he could fit in. The fact that he would eventually create and run a global furniture empire was not something that involved fate or luck, it was an active choice Ingvar made from a young age. Through dogged and stubborn work, he built up a company that reflected his personality and his dream. Nothing about IKEA's success was based on chance; it was based on attention to detail and sticking to the dream.

Example:

Kicking a ball is something that most people can do, but what sets David Beckham, the renowned soccer legend, apart from the rest of us? He has a pair of legs, two arms and a right foot – like most of us. The difference is what he did with that foot. Dedicated training, a good lifestyle, discipline, all the small things added up to his success – none of which included luck.

Advice:

To advance in life, things must change, nothing happens automatically. If things are working for you, do not change them – just ride the wave. However, if you are not satisfied with the road, you are on, exchange old habits or ways for new ones, and remember – everything you do, or cause, has a ripple-effect down the line.

Eye-opener:

If you are overweight, what is the best way to drop it? Is it by doing the same thing that made you overweight? Obviously not.

If you change where and how you invest your energy, you will see the results. This applies to all changes, large and small. Perhaps this also applies to thought-energy – in other words, what you focus your mental energy on eventually becomes reality, good or bad.

Charity and Goodness

There are some popular sayings which can be interpreted to mean the same phenomenon.

You get what you give.

You reap what you sow.

Be to others as you would like them to be to you.

"You will get all you want in life, if you help enough other people get what they want." - Zig Ziglar

What these phrases impart is that if you are friendly and helpful to others, the world tends to reciprocate.

The reason why this is so important in our search for wealth and happiness is that we want to create as much positive energy around us as possible. When we talk about receiving, we are really talking about being receptive to all the wonderful opportunities that come our way. If you radiate helpfulness, gratitude and goodness, people and events will be attracted to you like kids to an ice cream stand. And because you attract these types of people and opportunities, your life and your projects will flow even better. Goodness is the lubricant that reduces friction in life. You simply cannot do too much good.

There is an interesting aspect to this theory; apparently it does not matter what good deeds you do, good is not measured by arbitrary values. For instance, freeing a trapped butterfly is as good as helping a lady cross the street, or mowing the grass for your neighbor. One thing, however, is important: what was your intent for doing the deed?

In my experience, if you are doing something for someone else just to gain their attention or gratitude or make them think well of you or some other short-term gain, you are missing the point about this subject. It needs to be sincere. Doing good, that is, providing positive energy to help others in their lives, should be done because you WANT to help them, not because you are looking for a kickback or some personal gain. One is authentic, the other is fake, it has an ulterior motive built into it, making it insincere help – and usually, it is quite transparent to others.

Maximum success with this theory comes when your helpfulness towards others is something that you practice both consciously and unconsciously, every day, 365 days a year. That is when you will reap the benefits from giving to the world.

Advice:
Make it a habit to do at least one helpful act every day that is solely for the benefit of someone other than yourself: whether a friend, family member or stranger. Do not expect any thanks for doing it. Do it because YOU want to do it – not because you need acknowledgement. You will feel good about it, I guarantee it, and that is all the thanks you will ever need.

Eye-opener:
Is it a coincidence that Warren Buffet and Bill Gates, two of the world's wealthiest men, give more money to charity than anyone else?

The Wave Principle

There are different ways to achieve success as an entrepreneur. This approach is particularly fast. I refer to it as the *Wave Principle* – the rapid spreading of something, like waves skimming across the ocean. This is not a new theory, but rather, a fundamental rule of the universe.

You may have heard the story of the Indian mathematician who was rewarded by a ruler with any wish he wanted. The mathematician told the ruler that he wished for a single grain of rice on the first square of a chessboard, followed by two more grains of rice on the next square, four on the following one, and so on, so that the number increased exponentially each time. Given that a chessboard has 64 squares, in the end, he would have had more grains of rice than existed in the entire world. This is the *Wave Principle* in practical application.

This principle embraces one of the most powerful marketing tools – word of mouth. It starts with one person who is happy with a service or product. That person then tells another, who in turn, tells others, and so on. The word spreads exponentially, wave after wave, and eventually, after maybe fifteen or more referrals, thousands are purchasing the product/service – all of it started by just ONE person.

A fundamental characteristic of this theory is that once it gets going and providing nothing interrupts the quality of the product or service being delivered, the dissemination is virtually unstoppable. Try stopping a wave rolling across an ocean – you cannot. With this principle in application, the wave takes on a life of its own and becomes part of the cultural or popular movement.

To successfully leverage this, you must figure out how to convert 1 to 2, 2 to 4, and so on, and once the process passes a certain threshold, the wave gains an inertia all its own.

Eye-opener:

The million-dollar question is this; how do you get a customer to recommend your service or product to another?

Advice:
The wave theory is in use all around us. If you can figure out how implement it for your business, you will become rich beyond your wildest dreams. Convert one happy customer to two, two to four, and so on – and watch it go.

Energy Conversion

We can all, to varying degrees, channel extraordinary amounts of energy for long or short periods. A good example is that of the autistic person, who, despite their condition, is capable of amazing things, such as learning the contents of an entire phone book or putting to memory complex things which an entire group of people could not do. Another example of focused energy is the mother who lifts a car by herself to save her child. These examples, based on actual events, reveal just how much potential we can harness if we want; none of which is explainable in terms of science and which suggests that there is a lot more to us than contemporary metric systems can measure.

Imagine if you could somehow harness that potential, not by chance, but by pure will? So, what is the secret?

Having studied about this phenomenon I concluded that the most logical explanation for these incredible achievements is the transformation and control, consciously or subconsciously, of different energies in our vicinity, which are then focused. For instance, when the sun shines, we feel its warmth and nurturing energy, and yet, if you focus that same energy with a magnifying glass, it can burn through solid wood in a matter of minutes. That is called energy-conversion.

This is not new news. Athletes do it all the time when they visualize and focus their energy on winning. Interestingly, most athletes also refrain from engaging in the act of sex just before an important competition. Why? Simply put, it takes a lot of energy, they lose focus, and following sex, the body produces a relaxing hormone which is not particularly conducive to optimum physical performance in a sporting competition.

Other instances where this principle is used, is in creative processes. Artists, of whatever type, often do their best works while experiencing an intimate or critical episode in their lives, such as falling in or out of love, experiencing a deep loss or crisis, or some other traumatizing incident. How many songs do we hear every day about love and lost love? Many great artists throughout history have suffered from traumatizing mental health issues. Van Gogh, historically one of the greatest artists of his time, being a classic example. From the perspective of the theory of energy conversion, this is by no means, coincidental. Under such circumstances, whether it intense love, the anguish of losing a loved one, traumatizing experiences of one kind or another, we have learned to focus our energy and potential into the creative task at hand – drawing on something deeper and more profound.

It is my belief, that if we learn to channel these energies - we can achieve incredible results. If that is the case on an individual basis, what could we achieve as a group! In answer to that question, consider a country, such as Japan, which was literally decimated at the end of World War II, crushed in the wake of two nuclear bombs that devastated it. Today, Japan is a leading technological and industrial nation. At some point, it decided, collectively speaking, to focus its attention on creative, rather than military visions, and it transformed a broken nation in a matter of decades to one of the leading nations in the world today. The same could be said of Germany, left utterly broken in the wake of

WW II, it is today, one of the top industrial and commercial nations of the world.

One of the main reasons why we have not explored deeper into this area is because the field of science has a terrible habit of rejecting anything abstract, that is, those things they cannot measure with calipers and a test tube. Even though there exist countless examples of people who unlocked tremendous potentialities, such as the child prodigy who can play Bach at five years of age without ever having studied it, and other amazing facts, scientists tend to classify such phenomena as merely paranormal, or a pseudo-science at best, again, because they cannot explain it within the parameters of their existing science.

Eye-opener:

Given that you can change your life to such an extent that miracles are waiting just around the corner, what does this mean?

Advice:

Do not underestimate the power and potential of focused and purposeful energy - it is just waiting for you to tap into.

The Power of Goals

When we speak of setting goals, I am referring to setting a direction, a cardinal point to aim for in one's life.

Too many people mistake this to mean that if they are simply working and making money to pay their bills, their mortgage, to support a family, their retirement pensions, and the occasional vacation, that this is goal setting. On some level, of course, it is, but that is not what I am talking about here. I am referring to setting goals to reach YOUR dreams.

I am sticking my chin out here when I say that of all the people I have coached or discussed the path to happiness and prosperity with, only about 1% of them had a clearly stated direction in life; and I include myself in that statement.

The beauty of goal setting is it does not require much from you. If you just follow the advice here, you will have taken a large step toward achieving greater happiness and prosperity.

Try this approach:

1. Sit down somewhere quiet, where you will not be disturbed, and think about how you want to feel in five years from now. Think about what you want to do in five years from now. Think about who you want to be in five years, as a partner, a friend, a fellow human being, etc. Feel free to think of each of these in such detail that you can visualize it.
2. Write your thoughts on a piece of paper, in as much detail as possible, and put it away in a safe place.
3. Every year, take out that paper and read it, and as necessary, supplement or modify it, but always with a focus on the same five-year visions.

This is a powerful step forward, placing your feet on the road to greater success.

Eye-opener:
In a basketball game, who has the best chance of scoring the basket? The player who sees the basket and is focused on landing the ball there, or the one who looks in the other direction?

Advice:
Just do it! You will not regret it.

Prioritization

According to the principle of Prioritization, it is not necessarily the one who makes the most effort that gets the best results, it is the one who prioritizes best and does so in the right places. The problem with this theory is that one cannot entirely foretell which events will have the most positive effects, so instead, we focus on doing small things which can ripple out and have bigger results.

One of the most well-known movements of this mindset is perhaps, *"Lean Production"*, developed and masterfully implemented by Toyota Corporation, making it one of the most successful car manufacturers in the world. With Lean Production, one focuses on isolating all the points of waste, that is, where are we losing time and money in the production process – and then fixing those points, small or large. The result is increased productivity and profit. That is not the only application of Lean Production, but it serves to illustrate the point, that by finding the places which can be improved upon, one can achieve the greatest leaps in the overall situation.

Here is an actual example of this theory in application. An engineer at a car manufacturer, was tasked to significantly reduce the weight of their car models, making them less costly to manufacture and more fuel-efficient. Did he focus on fixing the large parts of the cars – the heaviest? No. He focused on the smallest, the nuts and the bolts, the things that hold everything together, of which, there were thousands in every vehicle. He figured out a way to remodel them, so they were smaller, and made of a lighter alloy, which in the end, resulted in reducing weight capacity of the entire vehicle by a large margin. This is an example of optimization and prioritization, and the power of small things having large effects.

The principle of Prioritization operates on this simple fundamental; by optimizing and prioritizing what you put your attention and energy on, there are absolutely no limits to what you can achieve.

This theory aligns to the principle known as the *Butterfly Effect*, which tells us that even the smallest of ripples, can have the most far-reaching consequences. The *Butterfly Effect* gets its name from the concept that a butterfly flapping its wings in Brazil, could ripple across the world resulting in a hurricane on the other side of the globe.

Eye-opener:
To achieve maximum speed towards wealth and prosperity it is critical that you prioritize your energy on those things or areas that will maximize results. The trick is to figure out what to prioritize, and then, to focus therein.

Advice:
Make a priority list of all the things you need to do to reach your goal. Start by stating the overall goal, and then list out all the things that you think will add up to achieving it. Then prioritize, focusing on the ones that will make the biggest difference – and remember, the small things can become waves for change.

The Power of Positive Thinking

If you focus on seeing all events as positive, where every event is either a new starting point in your life continuum, or at the very minimum, a boost, this perspective will have a huge impact on your future.

Two people buy a lottery ticket. One thinks to himself, *"I can win, I have a chance"*, while the other thinks, *"It's probably a waste of my time and money."* Which one do you think has the best chances of winning that lottery, the one who has the positive attitude or the one who buys the ticket but thinks it will make no difference?

Here is an all-too typical example. You are standing in a crowded room, possibly a pub, a party, wherever, and you see a stranger you are attracted to. If you are positive about the moment, you might think to yourself, *"I'll go over and introduce myself, maybe we like each other."* The happy marriage you dreamed of could be waiting right around that corner. On the flip side, if you have low self-esteem and fail to see or grasp the opportunity, and instead, you are compelled by some fear of rejection deep inside, the door is closed to you before you ever reach it.

I cannot stress enough how important it is to look at things positively. Even a terrible event in a life can be the beginning of something new. It all depends on how YOU respond to it. If you see it as negative, it remains so; but if you accept what has happened and see through it, to the other side, where your path continues, then the sun shines brighter.

One comment on feelings and emotions. If you have a feeling, you have it, you should it, and by doing so, emotions will come and go. You can learn to effectively navigate through the emotional waters and steer your life towards the more positive side. Do not bother trying to avoid or dismiss the feelings you feel about things, just become the master of HOW you deal with them – that is the secret to greater happiness and success.

When you become a master at seeing positivity, you will find that you are almost always happy and rarely angry or irritated. Sometimes there will be emotional roller coaster rides – just ride them out, because if there is one bedrock of truth you can count on, it is that life will go on, and it is entirely up to you HOW that goes.

Eye-opener:
Viewed from the perspective of the theory of positive thinking, nothing that happens in your life marks the end, but rather, the beginning of something new, or the affirmation of your goals.

Advice:
It does not matter what happens to you. What matters is what you do about it and the choices you make. Just remember, positive people move forward, negative sit in the past with their heels dug into the dirt.

Is "good" the enemy of miracles?

Many people accept that a "good" or mediocre result is enough.

If the goal is to reach Mars, then only getting to the moon is not good enough – it is a compromise.

Example:

Let us say that you are pharaoh of Egyptian times, one who invests fifteen years of time and immense resources to build a relatively small pyramid, but one which is nice to look at. The pyramid fulfills a function, and you are quite satisfied with it.

However, the construction has used up so much time and resources that you cannot perform any other great works during you reign. Perhaps you can erect another similar pyramid later, but you will never go down in history as the great pyramid builder. You will be remembered as the pharaoh who built "good" or mediocre pyramids, but certainly not the builder of world wonders, miracle structures.

Later, an equally rich pharaoh comes along, and he decides not only to build a pyramid, but to build one of the seven wonders of the world, a massive imposing structure. He plans, he conserves resources and then puts his whole soul into the project. Forty years later his structure goes down in history as one of the greatest ever.

A more modern example:

Someone comes up with the idea of creating IP telephony and starts a company that sells these services. He provides the service at a small cost and estimates sales at five hundred subscriptions in the first year, a thousand subscriptions the next year, and so on. A company is born.

Another entrepreneur comes along a year later and he thinks much bigger. With the wonder and imagination of a child, he believes that he can create a computer program that will change the world. After a lot of thought and planning, he concludes that this computer program must be free, easy to use, easily accessible and so on. Just like that, Skype is born, a software used by more than

100 million people today and a company that is valued in the billions of dollars.

In both examples, the conditions were the same, but the results differed because the attitude towards the projects was different. One was aiming for good, the other was aiming for the stars.

What these examples illustrate is that to reach beyond mediocrity, you must aim for something greater, you must aim high.

Eye-opener:

Good can become the best, but only if one keeps an eye on the latter, because aiming for "good" rarely achieves the best result possible.

Advice:

Decide to build a miracle and keep that vision.

Responsibility - the Key to Success

It cannot be stressed enough that if you want to be successful and happy in your life, and if you want to reach your dreams, then you must accept the fact that YOU are 100% responsible. Denying one's authorship or blaming others for your life or for any aspect of it, or in any way attempting to escape responsibility, will fracture your personal development and progress faster than just about anything.

The word responsibility comes from Latin, *responsum*, which means *to reply* – in other words, YOU are accountable, you are answerable – you are replying, not someone else.

There is no half-way when it comes to responsibility. If you are an engineer building a bridge or a skyscraper, you cannot be half responsible for it, otherwise, there is a good chance the structure will fail to stand up one day and people will not be pointing fingers at the weather, god, or anyone but YOU.

Responsibility is a one-way street, and if you accept it, then you accept full control of your life. You are no longer a victim of circumstance. You no longer assign blame to others. You realize that life is not about luck or bad luck. It is simply a question of assuming full responsibility for YOUR life. When you take responsibility, you are in control, YOU decide where you want to go, how you want to behave and react to things that happen in your life. It does not mean that negative things will not come your way, because life has storms and unseen pitfalls which are beyond your control, but how you react to them, whether you continue to navigate your ship through the stormy seas and do not quit, is the difference between the successful and the unsuccessful.

There are those who go through life with blinders on and who are "happy" to live it that way. People who avoid taking responsibility always seem to find someone else to pin the blame on for everything in their lives, whether it is the politicians, their neighbors, their boss, their parents, the police or maybe even the weather. The apparent "advantages" of shunting responsibility, however, denies one the real beauty of life, and all the dreams waiting to be met.

Eye-opener:

If you slip and fall on a wet lawn, is it the fault of the lawn, the shoe manufacturer, or your failure to have properly estimated the wet conditions you were dealing with?

On this point of responsibility, which person makes the best leader, and for that matter, someone you would follow? The one who accepts responsibility, or the one who pins it on others? Which would you feel more confidence and trust in following?

Advice:

Responsibility and success go together. Conversely, irresponsibility is the road to failure.

Never blame others for your condition or life.

The great benefit of taking responsibility is that you become much more aware of the risks and consequences, which in turn leads to significantly better risk-analysis, which ultimately leads to better decisions about your future.

The value of change

Those things which do not change or evolve over time usually eventually disappear.

In the realm of the business world, those companies that failed to adapt to a changing marketplace or new technology, became redundant or no longer needed. We have all seen them come and go, not just the small businesses, but even the giants.

Blockbuster Video is a great example. Blockbuster was the global video giant throughout the 1980s and 1990s. A massively successful company that was to be found most everywhere. Today, they are gone. Why? Blockbuster failed to adapt to changing technology and the fact that videos, and even CDs, were on the decline, and that new technology, livestreaming, was about to become the new kid on the block. They did not adapt, they did not change, they did not modify their platform or strategy, so a new upstart, Netflix, came along, and with better delivery, less overhead and a smarter idea, they left Blockbuster in total bankruptcy in a matter of years.

Darwin's teachings claim that the weak and least adaptable species eventually die. Whether this is true or not, the concept has some credibility when applied to the business world. Take IBM, once the business machine giant that missed important steps in computer development and evolution, losing them their dominant spot in the market to other companies, such HP, Dell, and Apple, who evolved and adapted with the times.

In all facets of life, there will always be someone who takes a step ahead in whatever field, whether it is setting a new athletic record, developing new technology, or devising new ways to do business. That is the nature of life, we are constantly evolving and reaching for new highs, and on the day, we cease to so create and settle into the rut of mediocrity, is probably the day we follow in the footsteps of Blockbuster et al.

In another sense, we have become the dominant predatorial species on the planet, and this same theory applies; if we do not change our ways and learn how to evolve with the planet we depend on, we will not have a world to live on in the future.

Eye-opener:

Who will survive best and has the best chances of reaching their goals – the one who thinks in terms of the long game, or the one fixated on short-term gains?

Advice:

Be as curious as a child about everything. Spend time with young people, look at life through their eyes and perspective, and learn from them and be prepared to share your experience and knowledge with them too. The younger generation is, by nature, better at change than you are. They are not set in their ways. Take advantage of this.

Minimalism

Living a minimalistic lifestyle should not be interpreted as depriving oneself of things, but rather, it should be viewed to removing many of the problems that consumerism brings with it. The biggest benefits of practicing minimalism are time, money, peace of mind and a higher standard of living.

Things take time.
All the things you possess come at a price – your time. A car must be maintained, a boat requires winterizing, and an apple tree needs pruning. If it takes ten minutes to do the boring thing that you "must do", that is ten minutes you will never get back. It is also ten minutes you could have spent doing something you love. Time is the most precious commodity we possess!

Material things cause concern
Possessions become an extension of you. If you have a boat in the water when a storm is coming, you will worry that it could be damaged. If you take your new sports car for

a drive, you will be concerned that something will happen to it. If you have a summer cottage unattended during the winter, you will wonder how the cottage is faring and whether everything is fine. Worrying about things taxes your power and inhibits focusing on the positive things.

Things get old

The minute you acquire a new possession, it begins to age – that is the nature of the universe. The latest smart phone is awesome for the first few months, until the newer model appears on the market, and then it is "old".

Personal example

I once purchased a jet ski. I was a diligent user and thought this was a lot of fun for the first year. In the second year, it was still fun, however, it began to lose its novelty. Towards the end of the second year, I began to see that the cost of owning the jet ski was questionable when compared to its value to my life and my happiness. I eventually sold it.

The bottom line is that jet ski came with its own baggage and a lot of additional expenses. It also caused concern because it was very prone to theft. The worst of it was that when newer models came out, it was less attractive to own the older one.

In the end, renting a jet ski, instead of owning one, provided me with the same pleasure, and it was less expensive in time, cost, and peace of mind.

When you think in terms of a minimalistic lifestyle, realize that you are not sacrificing a quality of life, nor are you living a poorer lifestyle. On the contrary, you are enriching your chances of success and true happiness by reserving your time, attention, and money for the important things.

Eye-opener:

Do you invest your time and money on those things that bring you closer to your goals, or are you spending time and money constantly raking the leaves?

Advice:

Think carefully before you acquire new things. They come with a price, and you must first make the decision; do you want to invest in the stuff, or do you want to invest your resources (time, attention, and money) into achieving your dreams.

The Law of Probability

The factor that "luck" will play in achieving your success and happiness is on the order of catching a leaf blowing by in a violent storm. What does play a role is understanding and using probability equations. I really want to point out how important and true this fact is, because successful people are almost always better at dealing with probability equations than those who are less successful. That said, the process is not always deliberately done, many times it is an unconscious process based on experience and events, but the fact remains that the better planned equation - the greater the chance of achieving the desired results.

"One-size-fits-all"

There is no one probability equation that fits everyone, all the time. Equations are a matter of personal assessment, followed by discipline and intelligence in their application.

For instance, a young woman decides she will become a top tennis player. She studies the game and the top achievers in this field. She determines what skills she must master to become a pro, and then comes up with a simple probability equation: A + B + C = D based on that analysis.

In this case, **A** represents how much time she must train every week; **B** represents how much coaching she will require weekly; and **C** represents the number of years she must train to perfect the art. In other words, **A+B+C = D** (Success).

The probability equation can be composed of almost anything, but it must be based on a correct assessment of what is required to achieve the stated goal, and it always includes time, discipline, and intelligent application. You will not get there by dreaming about it – success comes to those who observe, plan, and execute – and who stick to the plan, the dream. Ask any top athlete and they will tell you the same.

Taking chances

You can bet on stocks, a foreign exchange deal or maybe invest in gold, but that is not necessarily the way to the great successes. If you want to be sure of becoming a winner, you should not gamble away your money. Of course, there is always the element of risk in anything, whether you take on a speculative investment or jump into a new relationship, there are always risks, and we accept a certain margin of such. And naturally, that margin includes having faith in oneself and one's decisions. As the old saying goes, "take the leap of faith" – just make sure in doing so that your probability equation includes somewhere to land so you can keep going.

Warning

Some people get caught up in the trap of over-analyzing things. It is human nature to look critically at life and isolate possible dangers – we are, after all, vulnerable creatures. As dark clouds form on the horizon, one might be deterred from their course, but remember, storms pass eventually. Success requires an element of perseverance. Ask any entrepreneur how many storms they survived before achieving the next threshold in their goals and they will tell you some hair-raising stories, I am sure of it. It is often the case that the road you walk to achieve challenging goals is the one that offers up the greatest rewards in the end. Personally, I am drawn to those seemingly unattractive and intractable projects as my next venture. The key is to find and add to its probability equation enough positive elements to keep the right spin on the ball.

Eye-opener:

Do you think a good poker player is constantly taking chances or do you think they are good at probability equations and reading their opponents?

Advice:

Many investments guarantee a certain return if you have done the homework. Do a thorough job of thinking through the project. Plan it out, discuss it with others, study the playing field - all before you invest – and determine the risk factor and build a margin for that too. This is using probability equations to map your road to success.

When you have done this enough time, you become proficient at a particular niche, and you will only need a moment to determine whether an investment is right or not – because you will know, your insight will kick in, and your conscious grasp of the elements involved will help you to visualize potential outcomes, good and bad.

The Cash Flow Quadrant

In Robert Kiyosaki's book, *Rich Dad Poor Dad*, he talks about *"the cashflow quadrant"*, wherein life is divided into four parts, (see the figure below). I highly recommend you read this book. A real eye opener. It should be emphasized that many of us live our lives in several different quadrants at the same time. Choosing where you want to be is incredibly important as the different pieces of the cake offer different conditions.

Let's break it down according to this theory:

Employee quadrant

Most people start their professional career in this quadrant. As an employee, working for someone else, you receive regular salary payments in exchange for your time and work.

The Cons of this quadrant

- In this quadrant you must pay taxes and your bills – first and foremost,

otherwise you get into legal trouble with the government and banks.
- You have little or no control over your pension money.
- Usually there is no control over what health care you will receive, trusting that the health-care infrastructure will catch you when you fall, assuming there is even a health-care net to catch you.
- Another major drawback is that it is difficult to control your working time and how much money you make, both of which are usually governed by trade union agreements and management.

The Benefits of this quadrant

- In general, the employee experiences less stress than the self-employed, entrepreneur or business owner. If you are an employee, you clock-out after eight hours, five days a week, and take your annual vacation.

- There is often little concern about pensions and health care. You simply put your faith in the system.

Self-employed quadrant

This is obvious – if you are self-employed, you carry all the weight of your business.

The Cons of this quadrant
- The onus, or the burden of the job, company, is all on you.
- As a self-employed person, it can be difficult to expand the business and make more money as you often hit a glass ceiling, that is, YOU can only lay so many bricks in a day.

Benefits of this quadrant
- You pay insurance and pension deposits before tax and you can often control when you want to work.
- Financially, it is a bit easier in this quadrant, as some of your costs are absorbed in the business costs, before taxes, which can make a big difference.

Businessman/Owner quadrant

A business owner is someone who has a company, small or large, that he/she can leave in the hands of employees to run.

Cons of this quadrant
- The ultimate responsibility for the company can be a great burden.

Benefits of this quadrant
- It is possible to earn unlimited amounts of money since the company does not rely on only you – you have employees who can drive it.
- How you manage the company and the people in it can make all the difference in the world. As Steve Jobs said:

"It doesn't make sense to hire smart people and then tell them what to do; we hire smart people so they can tell us what to do."

- The opportunity to help other people, offer them jobs, give them more responsibility and let them develop are much better when you are a businessman.

Investor quadrant

As an investor, you use other people's time, money, and knowledge to advance your endeavor. The potential return is infinite, since one is not limited by your money, time, or knowledge – you have an entire world to invest in and play with.

Cons of this quadrant
- If incorrectly done, the risk is obvious, and it will backfire a thousandfold. It can be a costly experience if you fail at it.

Benefits of this quadrant

The opportunity for success is unlimited. The sky is the limit – but in today's age of space travel, even that is no hindrance.

Eye-opener:

Which of these four quadrants do you find the wealthiest people?

Advice:

Knowing how the different parts work and interplay with one another, and adapting your approach, accordingly, will take your life to new heights. And of course, read Robert Kiyosaki's book, *Rich Dad Poor Dad,* to get a full understanding of how to use the theory for success.

When are you rich enough?

Why is it important to determine the answer to this question? Isn't it just a matter of putting a number there?

Not really.

There are boats for hundreds of millions of dollars out there, and large archipelagos you can buy. If you put a figure on what you consider as "being rich", you will never be completely satisfied, either because you will be constantly chasing after that number, or the figure will be too low, which is also not good as it can hinder personal development.

For all those who set the goal of "getting rich", it is important, to have a distinct goal for their endeavor. It must be measurable, otherwise it is not a good goal and just pulling a figure out of the air is too risky and unnecessary.

Being rich is NOT just about achieving massive income, nor is it about having millions in the bank. What I can truly recommend is that you strive to achieve a solid passive income which covers your expenses and lifestyle.

Wikipedia defines passive income as:

Passive income is income that requires little to no effort to earn and maintain. It is called progressive passive income when the earner expends little effort to grow the income. Examples of passive income include rental income and any business activities in which the earner does not materially participate.

As an analogy, a steady stream of water can supply your needs just as well as a massive river. Whether it is ten thousand or a hundred million in annual income does not matter; the important thing is that you are free of the yoke which demands that you MUST work. Being rich is more about spending your time and earnings on what you want, and that determines "how rich you need to be".

Another reason for not setting goals only in terms of dollar value is that if you aim to become a good investor, you are quite likely to surpass your wildest dreams after a short time.

Eye-opener:
Who is most likely to become wealthy - the wasteful actor or the strenuous nerd?

Advice:
Make use of this definition for wealth. How rich you are is determined by how long you can last on your saved money and assets - without working.

Being debt free

I am convinced that our whole quest to get better is about getting our energies, our desires, call it what you will, all pulling in the same direction. If the goal is to get rich, the ambition must be to feel rich, act rich and think like a rich person; and to that end, I can say that rich people also do not accumulate debts.

If you buy one thing against an invoice, you generally have 30 days before it needs to be paid. Those 30 days are a loan from the seller. Since we want to act the part of being rich, we do not want to borrow, which means that rich people pay the invoice on day one.

If rich people are going to buy beds or televisions, they never take loans, and they rarely lease or take special offers, such as, *buy today and pay in three years.*

On the rare occasion that you must borrow money to achieve your dream, always pay it back as soon as possible – being in debt and being rich are diametrically opposed concepts.

Being indebted to someone or some agency, has morphed over the years from being bad and distasteful, to now, in our credit-card-obsessed culture, as perfectly normal, necessary, and even good. If you want to be rich, you will need to shake off that coat and put on a new one, the one you OWN.

If you are in debt, you are not free, because someone still owns a part of you; most likely your time, time needed to pay back the loan at interest and amortization.

Just because it says your name on the purchase contract for your house does not mean it is _your_ house. If you have borrowed money to buy the house, it remains the bank's house, a fact which becomes painfully real when you fail to pay the monthly mortgage, and they show up at your doorstep to reclaim it.

It is only when you are debt-free that you can really start living as a free person.

Eye-opener:

Who ultimately wins: the one who lends money or the one who borrows? The answer explains why banks are the wealthiest institutions in the world.

Advice:

Make the money first – then spend it - if you must.

The right tools

Once you have thought about what to go for in your life, it is time to look at the skills required to get you there.

It is vital to have the knowledge BEFORE you set off on a course of action. Most people would never attempt to fly a plane without learning how to do so first. It is the same with most any goal – you are investing your time and your money, and once the wheels are off the runway, you should know how to fly it and land it too.

The authors of the book, "*From Good to Great*" discovered that successful companies first searched out what knowledge and skills were available and only then decided in which direction they should go. In other words, it was not the blind leading the blind – they knew exactly what they were doing and where they were going.

Eye-opener:

What are the odds that you already possess all the knowledge necessary to succeed without doing any more homework?

Advice:

Working against the ocean currents will not get you far if you're training to sail from point A to point B. However, if you learn the skills of how to properly sail and how to navigate the waters, you will know how to leverage those currents to your advantage. It is the same in business and in life. Do not work against the energies and people around you. Look at what they want and what they can do and then decide what you are going to do and how you are going to accomplish it within the framework of those dynamics.

The positive debt

There is something I refer to as a *"positive debt"*. A positive debt is when you borrow money and use it to achieve a greater return. A positive debt is paid back as fast as success occurs. It does not lead one deeper into debt, but quite the opposite, it gets one closer to the intended objective. It may be in the form of bringing in venture capital or borrowing for real estate transactions or other types of loans and liabilities.

Example:
If you borrow money to buy an apartment building, which then results in more income than the interest on the loan and the upkeep of the property, you have created a positive loan, positive because the annual return will be greater than the costs, including the loan, which you can then pay back.

Let us say you make the same deal, but the interest on the loan and costs of upkeep exceed the revenue. In that case, you have created a negative debt, because you lose money every year and you still owe on the initial debt.

The big difference between negative and positive debts is that the positive one produces more money than it costs. The more positive the loan, the more return you get, and that would be a stable business model. Negative debts are a sieve to your wallet. Avoid them.

Eye-opener:

If you are currently borrowing money to invest in your projects, ask yourself, *is the return going to be positive or negative?*

Advice:

Aim to create positive loan scenarios – with a good margin of return. That is the road to success.

Finite Resources

Finite resources are those elements, which over time, become or will become, scarce or run out.

Oil is an example.
Diamonds another.
Forests yet another.

They are exhaustible resources – they do not last forever, and if this is not factored into equations and overall productivity, companies, or businesses or even ideas launched today, will not necessarily be around in the future when their platform disappears. Of course, when resources become scarcer, prices go up, and this affects all the players and consumers as well.

With global warming, we all know that our resources are finite. The days of careless waste, gutting out the Earth and polluting it in the process, are over – our survival demands it. We must find a balance where we do not consume the Earth's resources at the expense of a world to live in.

One thing we can be certain of, is that over the years to come, as Earth's population grows, as the demand for goods and consumerism increases, we must think with the "finite factor" if we are to succeed as a race, and not ruin our planet while doing it.

Eye-opener:

A hundred years from now, do you think the oil companies will be even bigger than they are today? Who has the best prospects of surviving? The one who plants the trees or those cutting them down?

Advice:

The future will remain bright so long as we deal with finite resources realistically and with care.

Feng Shui

Wikipedia defines Feng shui as follows:

Feng shui (Chinese: 風水), also known as Chinese geomancy, is a pseudoscientific traditional practice originating from ancient China, which claims to use energy forces to harmonize individuals with their surrounding environment. The term feng shui literally translates as "wind-water" in English.

Feng Shui can help one become more focused on the joy and love in life, and acts as a constant reminder of what direction we have set for ourselves.

In the West, the term Feng Shui is commonly used with reference to home furnishings; but in the East, it is a way of life.

If you follow the theories and advice provided in this book you will more closely approach the doctrines of Feng Shui. If you decide to look more closely at Feng Shui, then I recommend looking beyond its application in home décor and other superficial claims. Learn the basic ideology. There is a lot to explore and a lot more to be gained from it.

Eye-opener:
What is the optimal time interval to be reminded about one's goals?

Advice:
Utilize symbols in your home and workplace which remind you of your goals and ambitions. Why not get a money dragon to help you stay focused and give it a prominent position in your home as a constant reminder of where you are going? Symbology can help you to live it, feel it, and eventually, be it.

The Life Cycle

Our lifecycle is about 80 years – give or take. 80 years amounts to 29,200 days, or 700,800 hours. Roughly speaking, 175,000 of those hours comprise our childhood, another 175,000 is used for sleep, which leaves about half of that time for the rest of life's activities.

Taken from that perspective, it is reasonable to conclude that one should spend the remaining time on what you love and on those things that are important to you. Life is far too valuable to waste on things you do not like doing, and in areas where you do not want to be. Naturally, there are times in all our lives where we must bite the bullet and endure things, we would prefer not to have to spend time and effort doing, but even so, one should keep one's eye on the mountain top and get back on that road as fast as possible.

Sometimes an event needs to become a memory before its value and the lessons to be learned from it, can be fully grasped.

There is nothing wrong with daring life, to challenge it, to be a little wild and crazy. What is the worst that can happen? Life is short, so it is better to step on the gas pedal and do more, not less.

Eye-opener:
If you do not love investing your valuable time in maintaining a garden, maybe you should not have one – it is that simple.

Advice:
Think about how best to spend the time you have been given. One never knows when it will run out.

Being in the Present

You can rush your way through a whole decade, even a lifetime, only to realize that you have grown ten or fifty years older without really experiencing the presence of life around you.

Go outside and feel the bite of a strong wind on your skin, the scent of salt in the air, and the song it sings to you. Experience it through all your senses. The more senses you use, the better you learn and the more you will get out of life.

There is an incredible difference between living a conscious life or one that is on autopilot, which many people do without even realizing it. When we are present, meaning, aware, we draw better conclusions and thus make better decisions.

The individual who is aware of their surroundings, not only feels better, but they are also truly more "there" than someone who is running on autopilot, and so, the decisions they make, and the interactions they have with others, will be more meaningful and certainly more successful.

Eye-opener:

Which carpenter will deliver the better product?

The one who sees trees as living things, who goes into the forest and selects the one for his project, who cuts it down, prepares the wood and then uses his skills to create something aesthetic that will please his customer? A craftsman who experiences all facets of the trade.

Or is it the carpenter who merely does it for the money; who looks for shortcuts, uses inferior materials, only thinks only of his benefits and who lives by the mantra, *"time is money"*?

Advice:

When you really feel life, with all your sensibility and soul, your decisions come from a deeper place, a more intuitive place that interplays with those around you, and the results are better. Feeling and sensitivity toward life is not an obstruction nor is it an abstraction, because it is through feeling that we experience and know, and that knowledge helps to guide us. Those with selective blindness, who refuse to look and see, who are running on autopilot, are denying themselves the fruits of living.

It is when you possess solid knowledge that you come to know how and where to take shortcuts, ones that in good conscience, will not impair the result. Mindfulness is a ticket to greater success, this despite any false ideas which are prevalent in our "do it fast!" and "do it quick" society of today.

Where the wind blows

With the principles I have presented to you, you start to feel the pulse of the world in a way that can be quite overwhelming.

The opportunities that come your way, the doors that open to you, can, metaphorically speaking, be like a wind blowing in, the wind that fills the sails of your boat and starts you skimming across the ocean to your next destination. It is the winds of life, new chances, new opportunity, new ways to experience and succeed. The trick is to take advantage of that zephyr – and that takes practice.

The main thing you must practice is to dare yourself and to trust yourself. One must be vigilant if the wind turns, and one must dare to act on this as well. Taking those winds of life, daring to follow them, and mastering them, is an incredible asset.

Advice:
When you feel the wind blowing, do not leave your boat moored at the dock, raise the sails, and ride the waves!

Health and Well-being is No. 1

Take care of yourself and your body in the best way possible. Your body is your temple. Good health ranks above all else. Without it, you are living with limitations.

Make sure to eat just enough food – not more than you need. Eat natural ingredients as much as possible and try to avoid processed foods where nutrients have been lost.

Research shows that a food intake at a lower level is optimal for a long life - so eat less than more.

With the right diet and training you get more energy and you become noticeably more alert, which of course, immediately gives more joy and happiness.

Training

Training provides well-being, and well-being can make us more visually appealing to the world. Cardio training and fitness can really change the way we live our lives. You look and feel better when your body is fully functional and strong. Moreover, when you look healthy, it can affect how the world sees you.

Eye-opener:

If you ask a sick, elderly, or dying person, what they most want in life at that exact moment, what do you think their answer would be – money or good health?

Advice:

In your equation for success and happiness, put your health first. If you are not feeling well, your personal, family and business life will reflect it.

A word on politicians

You have a goal; you want to make a better society, city, nation, you want to make a difference and you decide the best way to do that is to enter the field of politics. Okay, then, let us project that goal with this narrative.

You join a party that has an ideology which you feel is quite close to your own values, and you begin the process of climbing up the rungs of that ladder, where your voice can have the most impact. Throughout this process, you do what a politician does, convincing people that you and your party are the solution to their problems, because in the end, you will only achieve that position of power, or remain there, by the goodwill of the electorate.

To achieve an influential political status within a democracy requires certain skills; for one, the ability to interact with people in a positive manner, such that you win them over to your camp; and moreover, the ability to navigate political waters, waters that are often filled with sharks.

Once you have achieved sufficient power within the party you represent, it is time to get even more power delegated to you. The electorate is a discerning group, they want to see results from those they elect to power, particularly results that benefit their lives, so you better be true to your campaign platform and provide results in whatever form benefits those who helped support you in your journey, or you will soon find yourself categorized as *"just another politician"*. This can be quick rewards, such as improved social benefits, tax reduction, improved pensions, better health care, etc. The categories are not that varied, because in the end, what the electorate is really looking for from their politicians is security and an improved life for themselves and their family. It is not rocket science, but it is very much about trust, transparency, and being predictable and consistent. If you say you are going to do something for them and they trust you to do it, then do it, because failure to deliver will begin to crumble your platform faster than you can imagine, especially in today's age of social media. And remember, personal goals aside, your entire purpose for existing as a politician, despite anything, is to serve the electorate. If you are there for any other reason, your disingenuous agenda will eventually be your undoing.

As a word of advice, just because you think that your platform is better or more righteous than your opponent's, does not mean that your voice will be heard or believed more than theirs, because in this field, you are in a boxing ring with others who have similar ambitions as your own, maybe even less sincere ones, where rhetoric is a powerful weapon – very often, more powerful than truth itself. Words are potent, and by the very nature of the political world, they can be the most powerful weapon in one's arsenal.

Like any profession, politicians must keep their own house in good order. A sloppy political platform, under-the-table dealings, and other unsavory circumstances detract from or completely hinder achieving the long-term goals intended to bring about a better group, municipality, city, or nation.

A food for thought:
If politicians had strived for the best long-term solutions, do you think the world would be the way it is today or would it be better?

Advice:
Politicians are no different than any other activity. They have a product to deliver to those who put them there, and they are only as good and valuable to the constituent as their ability to deliver that product. Words are cheap – results are what count.

When are you there?

This is a difficult question to answer, considering that we are, by nature, seekers, and our evolution and change never stop.

It is important to see yourself in the larger framework. The moment that you come to see that you are a small part in a large world, is the day you have achieved a big step in your journey. This is not to say that you are unimportant, or that your relevance is insignificant, it is only to say that the road to achieving greater happiness and success starts with acceptance of where you stand – and from there, you can start climbing the mountain to reach your goals.

My personal reflection is that you are close to your goal on the day when you feel completely at ease with life. The day when it is as fun to go to work as it is to practice one's hobbies or have a coffee with friends.

Assuming your finances have kept pace with your adventures, you are now fully ready to face the challenges of life.

I hope this book helps you to find your own path to happiness and success, and maybe, it inspires me to write book two. ☺

Sincerely,
Niklas Alm

www.ingramcontent.com/pod-product-compliance
Lightning Source LLC
Chambersburg PA
CBHW070236220526
45465CB00004B/1438